ADVANCE PRAISE FOR
Storytelling in Cambodia

"Willa Schneberg takes the reader on an extraordinary journey—from the Ramayana and Angkor Wat to the terrors of Pol Pot—encountering along the way Buddhist pacifism and the divine warrior, André Malraux and Tricky Dick and Kent State among a host of characters. Her Cambodia is a world and she's gotten deep within its skin. This is richly rewarding poetry, a compassionate, visionary response to a very real world."

—Sam Hamill

"At their best, these poems are intimately, despairingly human, with fabulous stories to tell."

—William T. Vollmann, author of *Rising Up and Rising Down*

"In *Storytelling in Cambodia* Willa Schneberg writes a searing account of one of the darkest moments in modern history. Schneberg's haunting verse testimony, her portraits of those who dragged a once peaceful country into the nightmare of genocide, her passionate homage to an ancient civilization now irrevocably lost move the reader even as they horrify."

—Carolyn Forché

"The poems in *Storytelling in Cambodia* record with sensuous, mindful detail a journey that is as geographically exotic and far-flung as it is spiritually profound. Ms. Schneberg combines first hand witness with Hindu myth to make poems which are by turns brutally documentary and lyrically elegiac, setting Cambodia's recent tragic history against the backdrop of its ancient past. This is poetry for grown-ups, written by a mature, even wise, human being."

—Peg Boyers, Executive Editor, *Salmagundi*

"*Storytelling in Cambodia* bears witness, in poem after poem, to the rawness of remembered passion. Willa Schneberg's poems about Cambodia, where she worked in the early 1990s for the UN, beautifully convey the sensuousness, excitement and uncertainty of a peculiar, tumultuous time. All of her poems take us with her as she catches often painful experiences in her hands like water from a tap and then transforms them, with transcendent skill, into creations that shimmer in the heat."

—David P. Chandler, author of *The Tragedy of Cambodian History*

"Willa Schneberg is a poet who boldly faces evil and has the courage to express her reactions as art and testimony. The wisdom underpinning her poems is fully earned. We need more such poets who are not deterred from writing about global issues by those who have neither the concern nor courage to do so themselves. This book will be controversial because it is out of step with the dominant aesthetic of our time, which elevates triviality to exalted ennui. Her elegy for Pol Pot catches the banality of evil as few writers have attempted."

—David Ray, author of *The Death of Sardanapalus and Other Poems of the Iraq Wars*

Storytelling in Cambodia

FOR JENNIFER,

WHO KNOWS
WE MUST CREATE

OCT 07

Storytelling in Cambodia

by
Willa Schneberg

CALYX Books
Corvallis, Oregon

Also by Willa Schneberg

In The Margins Of The World, Plain View Press
Winner of the 2002 Hazel Hall/Oregon Book Award for Poetry
Box Poems, Alice James Books

Publication of this book is supported in part by grants from The Autzen Foundation; the Oregon Arts Commission and the National Endowment for the Arts, a federal agency; the Edna L. Holmes Fund of the Oregon Community Foundation; the Spirit Mountain Community Fund; and the generous support of Floyd and Beverly McFarland, Nancy Nordhoff, and Charles B. Katzenstein.

Cover art: photo by Willa Schneberg
Cover and book design by Cheryl McLean

CALYX Books are distributed to the trade through Consortium Book Sales and Distribution, Inc., St. Paul, MN, 1-800-283-3572. CALYX Books are also available through major library distributors, jobbers, and most small press distributors including Baker & Taylor, Ingram, and Small Press Distribution. For personal orders or other information: CALYX Books, PO Box B, Corvallis, OR 97339, (541) 753-9384, FAX (541) 753-0515; www.calyxpress.org.

⬯

The paper in this book meets the guidelines for permanence and durability of the Committee on Production Guidelines for Book Longevity of the Council on Library Resources and the minimum requirements of the American National Standard for the Permanence of Paper for Printed Library Materials Z38.48-1984.

Library of Congress Cataloging-in-Publication Data
Schneberg, Willa
    Storytelling in Cambodia / by Willa Schneberg
        p. cm.
    ISBN-10: 0-934971-90-0 (pbk. : alk. paper) : $13.95.
    ISBN-13: 978-0-934971-90-4
    1. Cambodia—Poetry. I. Title.
PS3619.C4466S76 2006
811'.6—dc22   2006001150

Printed in the U.S.A.   9 8 7 6 5 4 3 2 1

ACKNOWLEDGMENTS

I would like to express my deep appreciation to poet and memoirist U Sam Oeur and poet and translator Ken McCullough for writing the introduction to this collection. Both authors have a profound relationship with Cambodia.

I would like to thank David P. Chandler, Elizabeth Becker, Rebecca Stefoff, Henry Kamm, Molyda Szymusiak, William Shawcross, and Alex Madsen, whose works on Cambodia and Southeast Asia provided invaluable resources. I also want to thank journalists Philip Shenon, Claudia Dreifus, and particularly Seth Mydans, the Southeast Asia Bureau Chief for the *New York Times*, for his trenchant coverage of Cambodia and Southeast Asia. Specific *New York Times* articles written by Seth Mydans inspired my poems "Elegy" and "Johnny Got His Gun."

I would like to thank Judith Arcana, Judith Barrington, Patrica Bollin, Peg Boyers, Elizabeth Claman, Angie Chuang, Ruth Gundle, Sara Halprin, Jana Harris, Betty Mandl, April Ossman, David Ray, Hannah Stein, and members of the Pearl Poets, past and present: Karen Braucher, Maggie Chula, Raphael Dagold, Christine Delea, Leanne Grabel, Jennifer Grotz, Judy Montgomery, Paulann Petersen, Cassandra Sagan, Penelope Scambly Schott, and Pat Vivian, all of whom offered essential critique in different ways. I wish to offer my gratitude to D.J. for her tireless efforts publicizing this collection, and to Sarah Lantz Woodside, without whose support this manuscript would not have been published.

Thanks also to Literary Arts, Inc. for the Walt Morey/Oregon Poetry Fellowship, to The Money for Women/Barbara Deming Memorial Fund Grant in Poetry, and to the Tyrone Guthrie Center at Annaghmakerrig, Ireland, where a number of these poems were conceived.

I would like to offer my respect and admiration to the staff at *CALYX*: Margarita Donnelly, Beverly McFarland, Cheryl McLean, Kathleen Bryson, Maureen Rhea, and others, for the care and professionalism they exhibited at every stage during the production of this volume.

I would like to thank my fellow United Nations Volunteers and the Khmers who worked with us in UNTAC for their commitment to freedom and democracy.

—

Grateful acknowledgment is made to the following publications, in which these poems were previously published: *American Poetry Review*: "Picturing Pol Pot," "The Locket"; *Americas Review*: "Eulogy," "You Know the Killing Fields," "Into My Office Walks Vietnam's Legacy"; *Blue Mesa Review*: "Phnom Penh as Still Life," "For Myo Myo: Horsecart Driver # 142"; *Bridges: A Journal for Jewish Feminists & Our Friends*: "You Know the Killing Fields," "Sunset in Hebrew and Khmer"; *Chaffin Review*: "On the Road with St. Paul"; *Clackamas Literary Review*: "Counseling in Phnom Penh," "Storytelling in Cambodia"; *Fireweed*: "Pol Pot's Wife Talks to Whoever Will Listen"; *Five Fingers Review*: "Absentee Ballot"; *The Grove Review*: "The Bat Collection"; *Illuminations*: "I Look in My Passport at the Triangle Stamped 27 Feb 1993," "Ode to a Gecko"; *Jacaranda*: "The Bells of St. Bavo Sing Scat"; *Jefferson Monthly*: "Ben's Shoes"; *Loyalhanna Review*: "Electric Can Opener"; *Manzanita Quarterly*: "The Anger Room"; *Michigan Quarterly Review*: "Prosthesis Maker"; *Mudfish*: "Interrogation," "Elegy"; *Nervy Girl*: "Ode to a Betel Chew"; *Omega*: "The Place Where Death Lives," "Off Screen," "Summer of the Secret Ballot"; *The Oregonian*: "Laryngectomy"; *Pearl*: "Grief"; *Poetry Now*: "Love Poem"; *Rosebud*: "What Is Left"; *Salmagundi*: "The Reaper," "A Cartographer's View of the World," "Chinese New Year"; *Silverfish Review*: "Hawthorne Bridge"; *West Wind Review*: "Accident on Achar Mean"; *Xanadu*: "Hanuman, Leap for Me."

Anthologies: "The White Whirlybird with the Black Letters Makes a Landing" and "What I Know" were published and "Absentee Ballot," "Chinese New Year," "You Know the Killing Fields," "Sunset in Hebrew and Khmer" were republished in *Passionate Lives: Eight Autobiographical*

Poem Cycles (Queen of Swords Press). "The Bells of St. Bavo Sing Scat" was republished in *Hard Love: Writings on Violence and Intimacy* (Queen of Swords Press). "Prosthesis Maker" was republished in *Points of Contact: Disability, Art and Culture* (University of Michigan Press). "Into My Office Walks Vietnam's Legacy" was republished in *Portland Lights: A Poetry Anthology* (Nine Lights Press). "The Hotel Cambodiana" was published in *Knowing Stones: Poems of Exotic Places* (John Gordon Burke Inc.). "The Locket" was republished in *Bearing Witness: Teaching the Holocaust* (Heinemann). "Grief" was republished in *Chance of a Ghost* (Helicon Nine Editions) and will be republished in *This Year's Best Fantasy and Horror: Nineteenth Annual Collection* (St. Martin's Press). "Pol Pot's Wife Talks to Whoever Will Listen" will be republished in *Regrets Only* (Little Pear Press).

To the Cambodian people for their courage,

and to my life partner Robin,

who would not let me stop sending out this manuscript.

—

CONTENTS

The Vow

Leaving Cambodia

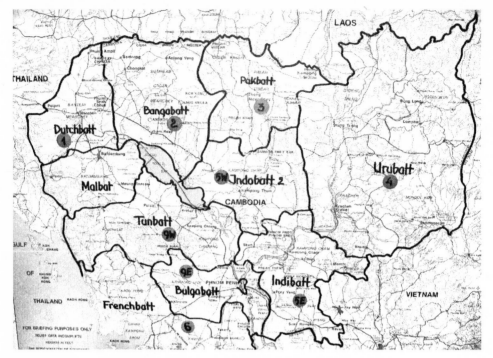

Cambodia Special UNTAC Map (Unofficial)

This map was given to me by a peacekeeping troop who served during the time of the United Nations Transitional Authority in Cambodia. The thick black lines do not divide up the country by provinces, e.g., Battambang, Kampong Som, but by areas under the auspices of U.N. peacekeeping troops from various member countries during the mission. For example, Frenchbatt (in bold letters) is the French battalion. Other countries represented are Bangladesh (Bangabatt), India (Indibatt), Indonesia (Indobatt), Pakistan (Pakbatt), Malaysia (Malbat), Uruguay (Urubatt), Bulgaria (Bulgabatt), the Netherlands (Dutchbatt), Tunisia (Tunbatt), and Ghana, which does not appear on the map. The numbers stand for different battalions. Malbat is not numbered.

Willa Schneberg

INTRODUCTION

I must admit that when I looked at the table of contents of *Storytelling in Cambodia* I was suspicious—but as I made my way through the poems it became immediately apparent that this was a rare book, not only in its scope and vision in general but in particular its grasp of Cambodian history and culture. I was suspicious because Americans often consider themselves experts on a place or a subject after the most cursory acquaintance. Yes, Willa Schneberg actually spent significant time in Cambodia, but her intuition has taken her far beyond what most people would have gleaned from that experience. From the outset, the poems in this book braid strands adeptly, which makes us wonder if and how Schneberg can sustain this magic. Her biography tells us she is a skilled potter—obviously she is a skilled weaver, too. Recent Cambodian history is usually presented as a tragedy, and one is tempted to be maudlin in writing about Cambodia, and to beat one's breast in indignation. Schneberg does not do this—she presents us with a tapestry of Cambodian life and history and her own ongoing life in context. It is a seamless fabric.

As I read this book, I was constantly surprised by her chutzpah—at tackling so many aspects of the subject that is and was Cambodia. In addition to the sources which Schneberg acknowledges, one is reminded of books (like Robert Bingham's *Lightning on the Sun*) in which American ex-pats get caught up in (and destroyed by) the Xanadu aspect of Southeast Asia—the Sean Flynn syndrome. Films featuring relationships with "The Other," like *Hiroshima Mon Amour*, *The Quiet American*, *Indochine*, and *Heaven and Earth*, and books like John Burdett's *Bangkok 8* also come to mind.

Schneberg acknowledges that she is not an insider, yet she gets convincingly inside the Cambodian mind and psyche. One tack she takes right away is to admit that, even though she is Jewish, she is *not* privy to the sufferings of the Holocaust, nor does she have an inside track to understanding and empathizing with Cambodians who experienced the auto-genocide of the Pol Pot regime followed by life during the ongoing Vietnamese-backed reign of Hun Sen.

In the opening section of the book, we come to see, implicitly, the actions of the Khmer Rouge prefigured in the violence of the *Ramayana*, the Hindu epic on which most of Angkorian tradition is based. But Schneberg also presents the sensuality of the *Ramayana*, and that thread is in evidence throughout the book. One is reminded of the *bhakti* poets of the Hindu tradition such as Mirabai, Muktabai, Kabir, and Surdas, poets for whom spiritual and physical ecstasy are indistinguishable. Dichotomies such as this abound: though he or she may be a pacific Buddhist, every Cambodian aspires to be the warrior depicted on the friezes of Angkor Wat.

In the second section, we are furnished with journal entries from Henri Mouhot, the "discoverer" of Angkor Wat—typical perceptions of a Euro-centric colonialist, who then, as he is dying of fever, undergoes a Conradian transformation. André Malraux is also revealed at possibly the lowest point in his life, when he and his wife were eventually apprehended after stealing pieces of the temple at Banteay Srei. As we know, Malraux went on to become an exemplary statesman.

In the next section, "Picturing Pol Pot," Schneberg reminds us that the tragedy at Kent State was the direct result of Nixon's bombing of Cambodia. She follows this with a poem about Sihanouk's cinematic endeavors. This juxtaposition sets the table for Pol Pot. At this point in the book Schneberg has already presented us with several stylistic shifts, but now discloses a message, verbatim, in broken English, from AP reporter Mean Leang, as the Khmer Rouge were taking over Phnom Penh. She will use found items throughout the book to startling effect. Another example, later in the book, is a list of advice for those who live in proximity to landmines. There are more landmines per capita in Cambodia, and more amputees as a result, than in any other country in the world. This is a subject about which it is easy to wax strident, but Schneberg makes it personal, tangible, by writing a piece from the point of view of a prosthesis maker.

Schneberg takes us out of Phnom Penh to the countryside under the Khmer Rouge, then back. Much of what happened under Pol Pot is undocumented, but most of us have seen the photographs from S-21. Schneberg uses the painter Vann Nath, one of the seven survivors, to ground this experience. She follows with a poem from the point of view of Pol Pot's first wife, Khieu Ponnary, who was driven insane, then a poem about Nhem Ein, who took most of the photographs, and a poem concerning Duch, the "jailer" at S-21, who, ironically, has undergone a "Road to Damascus" conversion to Christianity. Within this sequence Schneberg has inserted a poem focusing on the women who developed permanent spontaneous blindness as a result of their experiences during Pol Pot's reign of terror. What we choose to see, what we are forbidden to see, what we are forced to see. And what it does to us.

In the section titled "Absentee Ballot," Schneberg gives us the landscape and climate during the time she was there, when UNTAC (United Nations Transitional Authority in Cambodia) was monitoring elections. We see, for example, the situation with landmines in abundance, the imbalances created by having overpaid outsiders present in a country rife with abject poverty, what it was like to work in that milieu and maintain a modicum of consciousness. Again, the contrasts. The brilliant beaches along the coast contrasted with the dump full of toxic substances, including medical waste. If you want to witness this firsthand today, go to the city dump on the outskirts of Phnom Penh, where young children spend their days picking through such waste and their nights sleeping atop mounds of compressed garbage. There is a poem titled "The Bat Collection," about collecting guano from the monuments of the past. One wonders who the bats symbolize, but it isn't too hard to figure.

The poet begins her leave-taking from Cambodia in the penultimate section of the book, "The Vow." We see life under other nearby repressive regimes, Burma in particular, and the poems have a somewhat hallucinatory quality. The persona in the poems is displaced and is still processing what she has learned—an echo of Henri Mouhot, but in a world much more complex though not in extremis. The protagonist is a sensualist, as she was at the beginning of the experience, but one senses that she is becoming more like the celestial *apsara*.

In the final section of the book, the poet is now removed from Cambodia physically, but not emotionally or spiritually. Cambodia is with her, whether she is in the Netherlands or at home in Oregon. Whether she is working as a therapist with a Vietnamese client or assessing her mother's laryngectomy. Whether contemplating the Hebrew characters she studied as a youth or the Khmer characters of her adulthood or, finally, seven years later, writing about her experiences with some distance, it is no accident that the final poem is set in Ireland, another country no stranger to oppression.

Who would have the wherewithal to synthesize all these elements in the same slim but substantial book of poems? You would expect it to be sprawling but it is not—because the connections are natural and earned. If one knows the history, then and now, the life on the street and in the village, *Storytelling in Cambodia* rings true, and it rings sonorously. I hesitate to say that Willa Schneberg has written a book with "global" implications, because that word has fallen into disrepute of late; I will say, instead, that she has written a book that is genuinely universal, from which all of us can take away valuable lessons. She is a profound, subtle, and talented teacher.

U Sam Oeur with Ken McCullough, co-authors of
Crossing Three Wildernesses
December 2005

Storytelling
in Cambodia

STORYTELLING IN CAMBODIA

After a cold shower,
both dripping wet,
she sits between his open legs
on the silky sheets of the hotel bed;
as he leans against the wall,
starting with her hair,
he touches her—
her face, her breasts,
her belly, between her legs,
until there is no wife
and only their afternoons.

Afterward, she sits in his lap.
He tells her stories and sometimes
she has stories to tell.
She never tires of the giraffe ones,
when in the land of banyan trees
he finds her, green-eyed and silver-spotted.
She had not yet forgotten language and
teaches him, *I love you*.

He repeats, *I love you, I love you, I love you*,
as he rocks her. But the story,
the one that will destroy everything,
she keeps to herself:

> *In the countryside a husband dissatisfied*
> *with his childless wife takes a lover.*
> *He meets her for trysts*
> *instead of going to the rice fields*
> *and soon he wants his wife to die.*

He asks his lover to go into the forest
to find a tree that houses a powerful spirit
who will kill the wife, but as she is begging
the deity to perform the deed

she hears his wife's voice pleading
with another godling to rekindle
her husband's fierce love—
once he looked at her face
and thought he saw his own.

The wife's love is as potent as hers;
she knows it. Tears flow from her eyes and
won't stop; her body becomes water—
she is a river looking for an ocean.

YOU KNOW THE KILLING FIELDS

for Rada Long, interpreter

She believes because I am Jewish
I must understand
what she went through after Cambodia
was ground down to zero on April 17, 1975,
when grim-faced teenage boys
wearing fatigues over black pajamas,
grenades, pistols, rifles, rockets
weighing down their shoulders,
marched cocky into Phnom Penh.

I must understand how the Angka found her
in the paddies in the moonlight stuffing rice kernels
into her pockets to keep from starving
and bashed in the back of her head with a shovel.

I must understand that they frisked her,
found the eyeglasses inside her *krama*
and smashed them into the monsoon-soaked soil, raving:
*Traitor, intellectual relic, you can't run from
the "Super Great Leap Forward"* and then slashed
her arms with the shards of broken glass.

I must understand why they threatened
to cut out her tongue for humming
a snatch of song sung by Sin Samouth,
the Frank Sinatra of Kampuchea,
who is nothing more to them
than a bourgeois capitalist pig
masquerading as a Frog.

I do not tell her I wasn't there,
that I read about the Holocaust like any goy
who wishes to understand.
Instead, I tell her about a Nazi who sat at a table
covered with delicacies and booze,
holding an automatic pistol in his hand,
who forced Jews to lie naked face down in a pit
and between shots of cognac shot them dead . . .
as if it were my story.
She says, *You don't know how happy*
you make me, you know the killing fields.

Note: Sin Samouth was lured back to Cambodia from
Paris to be a leader in the "revolution" and was then
murdered.

THE LOCKET

*Dr. Haing Ngor survived the Pol Pot time pretending
to be a taxi driver. He won an Academy Award for
playing Dith Pran in the film* The Killing Fields.
He was murdered in Los Angeles on February 25, 1996.

If what they say is true
about the locket,
Haing Ngor died for love.
He was found slumped over near his Mercedes,
not unlike the one he owned in Phnom Penh
before Pol Pot had his way with the country;
Ngor would not let the thugs take the gold locket
with the only picture that remained of his wife,
the one he stole back from the Khmer Rouge puppet
who snuck into his shack looking for his wife's jewelry
after Huoy crossed the sea.

He would have suffered the vise's spikes on his forehead again
and the endless pinging of water in the center of his temple
if he could have stopped them
from ripping off his neck
the talisman of his wife
that he always wore
behind his clothes, next to his skin.

Huoy died in childbirth, too malnourished to feed the fetus.
Haing's doctor's hands could do nothing but cradle her
as she stopped fighting the hunger,
his black bag empty.
If Haing Ngor had performed a miracle
and the baby slid out of her tired body,
Angka bullies would have shoved
the tears of the two still alive
back into their eyes
before kicking them into the earth's moist belly.

Afterward, he buried her in two silk outfits,
so she would have a change of clothes in paradise.
Then he did what only widows do:
He shaved his head and wailed
like a wife for her dead husband.

HANUMAN, LEAP FOR ME

In the Ramayana, *Hanuman leaps into Lanka to save Sita.*

Monkey face, with eyes the color of wilting forsythia,
even as an infant the world was your rattle,
the sun your papaya.
You jumped toward its fire
until your father The Wind left the sky breathless
and whisked you away
to safety in the cave.

Master of the prank,
what about your escapade
when you saved the life of the princess
you hardly knew, out of duty, not love?

Now I want you to leap for me—
for the silent one with a dark computer screen,
the distracted one whose grogged clay never found a wheel,
the disenchanted one whose heart never flew from her chest.

Leave the gods behind on Mt. Meru and leap,
and while you are at it:
Suck birds of paradise and lotus petals into the sky,
unmingle sea lions on huge boulders and
hurl them into the clouds and make
underwater volcanoes cream again.

Fling yourself off that mountain of immortals.
I'm right here, baby,
leaning over the side of the divan
poised to catch you, waiting
to wrap my pale limbs
around your thick white furry loins.

DESIRE

In the Ramayana, *the demon Maricha
transforms into a golden stag.*

I

It is my fate to be the bait to catch Sita.
Ravana has more wives than his twenty arms
can handle, but of course he wants doe-eyed Sita,
star of earthly beauty
whose black hair hugs her ankles.

As Ravana passes me the coconut shell
brimming with wine,
I stop trying to dissuade him
from using my legerdemain.

I am a homely giant.
When women gaze at my smirking face
they feel disgust,
but I will die adored.

II

Without a voice I will not sound common.
My face will be sapphire blue.
My calves slender as the legs of *apsaras*.
My ivory antlers tipped with moonstones,
my hooves glossy black,
my eyes violet amethysts and
my hide golden.

Entranced by my beauty
Sita will beg Rama to catch me.
I will be translucent, glowing
around the edges, exquisite.

Trapped by desire
he won't see my grotesque form
until his golden arrows pierce my heart.

The Anger Room

In the Ramayana, *Kaikeyi learns her son was not chosen to be king.*

When green coconuts still clung to the tops of trees,
pressed their cheeks against one another and
listened to the call of Garuda, the bird king,
and before the moon blocked the sun,
I was in bed eating mangoes
the shape of tear drops,
the color of fire,
flamethrowers swallowed for my pleasure.

But now I am in the anger room
tearing my clothes and weeping.
Uncut rubies once docile in a silk sack
are now daggers in my back.
I writhe against them
in the body loaned to me,
the flesh Dasaratha owns.

Once, years ago, I was allowed to leave the palace.
Dasaratha was fighting against the Asuras of Drought.
He was wounded so badly his blood
trickled into my scalp matting my black hair.
I grabbed the reins of the sky chariot
flying us to safety.

I guess there was always a fist inside me.
I will lunge like a cheetah if my son Bharata falls prey to fools.
For years I purred and yawned, but in this dank room
the King will hear me growl and come to me.

If he makes Kausalya's son king, I will claw
his soft Royal face, but he wouldn't dare.
My fury will freeze his force
and he will do as I say.

SITA HAS HER SAY

Shabby Valmiki, your beard long as imagination,
your garments old as language,
thanks for the offer,
but I will not remain here
inside your house of leaves.

Although you believe
you are my father and the father of poetry,
I want nothing from you.

Yes, you made me beautiful, but spring soon turns to winter.
I'm sick of your description of the curve of my eyebrows,
the softness of my throat, the fullness of my breasts.

How dare you imprison me in Asoka Grove
guarded by Rakshasas with upside-down noses, cow legs,
and voices that screech: *Give yourself*
to Ravana or we will eat you with sauce.

Why did you force me to deal with the monster himself
when he has hundreds of long-lashed women
wearing sheer silks stitched with tiny bells
curling into each other on the floor of his bedchamber?
Since you made him want me,
I knew he would let me live,
but I had to put up with his fits,
rolling his twenty red eyes and shaking
his hundred fingers in my face.

Why did you make my beloved Rama loathe me?
During my thirteen years of captivity
simply imagining touching his dark-green hair again
kept me from suicide.
But when you finally reunited us,
you hid the truth of my chastity from him.
He, who gazed into my eyes
when I awoke in the morning and
dropped off to sleep at night, could no longer
bear the sight of me.

I asked Lakshmana to build a pyre.
He dragged logs and kindling onto the palace's marble floor.
Rama did not stop him.
I thought I could not live without Rama's love.
If I'm impure, let the flames take me, I said.
The fire stripped my sari from me.
I felt frozen as if clothed in snow and knew
I did not need to prove my chastity to you,
to Rama, or anyone.

When I emerged unsinged, the sound of shell trumpets
and lutes filled the air and garlands were strewn
from my feet to my husband's throne.
He ran toward me, his arms outstretched.
I refused to turn around.
I covered my nakedness
and left forever
to live where women can tell their own stories.

THEIR FATHER

Kusa and Lava are Rama's sons.

The boys are always asking about their father.
I don't tell them he saw me
as nothing more than a gaudy locket
waiting to be opened.

I tell my sons what they should hear—
their father spends days shooting golden arrows,
speaks all languages including bee and buffalo,
and knows inside his subjects' hearts.
I don't say my heart is a pomegranate,
its many seeds left embedded,
unsucked between their father's teeth,
his mouth unstained with red.

Before they sleep tonight
again they want me to tell
how their father came to claim me.
No one could even lift Shiva's bow out of its iron case,
or draw it back, except your father.
He pulled so hard, it broke in two.
Now go to sleep.

I have burned my copies of the *Ramayana*.
If I can just keep my boys underground,
they will never meet the scoundrel Valmiki
and learn of my betrayal—

of how Rama listened to the gossips and
snared by the thought of other men touching my body
abandoned me in the woods near the Ganga,
his sons in my belly.

My mother, who usually lets fate take its course,
lost her patience,
broke the earth open, and
made a deep chasm,
then rose from the bowels of the earth
on her throne of roots and stone
to hold me bawling in her lap
and took me home.

The Sea of
Churning Milk

TO THE MEMBERS OF THE ARCHEOLOGICAL SOCIETY OF LONDON

After a letter by Henri Mouhot
Ongcor, Cambodia, 4th April, 1860

Dear Gentlemen,

It seemed like yesterday when I was traveling
in grand style with an amiable mandarin
who had been to Laos to fetch the Great White Elephant.
These people are very superstitious and believe the soul
of some prince or king passes into those lumbering creatures.
The elephant dined on gold dishes,
devouring an inordinate amount of cakes, biscuits,
and sweetmeats, then died of indigestion.

When I journey through a town in my tropical costume,
go to the market or a pagoda, I am a curiosity.
People crowd around and stare and keep staring
in complete silence until I am a speck in the distance,
as if I were a god-incarnate given to destroying the rice crop
or making barren women fertile.

My dear friends, tonight I am not writing
to detail my travails in this savage land.
As you know, my specialities are entomological and conchological.
Although my desire is not to impose my opinions on anyone,
I do believe I have stood before the greatest monument
the ancients have left us.
When I am again in your esteemed company,
I wish to present a paper illuminating my observations
on these astonishing ruins.

But this evening, writing by the light of a torch,
sitting on an ape skin newly stripped from its carcass,
next to a box of insects requiring preservation and labeling,
I wish to tell you how I became overcome with emotion,

captured by the magnificence of the magestic Ongcor—
the greatest temple ever erected to their gods.

I and members of my party were on foot
in this torrid zone. Even the natives could not bear
contact with the steaming ground; the oxen refused to stir;
the water in the green lotus ponds scalded our lips.
On the brink of exhaustion we carried on
pushing our way through the nearly impenetrable jungle,
until a splendid edifice appeared before us
with five conical towers and a grand promenade,
rivaling the temple of King Solomon.
Miraculously my fatigue vanished, my spirits soared.

The present day inhabitants of Cambodia
are an inferior lot. I believe them incapable
of erecting a monument with the grandeur of the Parthenon.
Perhaps Khmer legend holds the secret.
Par-Eun, the leprous Angel King, may be the designer
or the god-giants who wear conical hats and
serene expressions while they haul massive stones.

But these primitives thrash missionaries with rods
and with each blow cut the flesh of our sainted men of God,
spilling their blood. Only when Queen Victoria or Napoleon
takes this god-forsaken place in hand
will something worthy of awe
rise anew toward Heaven.

Your Humble Servant,
H. Mouhot

Note: Henri Mouhot has been credited with being the first European to "discover" Angkor
after it was sacked by the Thais in the fifteenth century.

DELIRIUM

*I candidly confess that I have never been more happy than when
amidst this grand and beautiful tropical scenery in the profound solitude
of these dense forests, the stillness only broken by the song of birds and the
cries of wild animals and even if destined here to meet with death I will not change my
lot for all the joys and pleasures of the civilized world.*
—M. Mouhot

*On 10th November, 1861 ... he was attacked by jungle fever
and died after twenty-two days of illness.*
—J. J. Belinfante

racked with chills
a glacier lodges in my body

Helix cambojensis—shell sinistral, deeply umbilicated, canoidly globose,
Bulimus camojiensis—shell dextral, cylindrically ovate, interior iridescent
violet-rose ... must record before ...

Bopha, Vannith, make preparations for the journey to Bana Kakau

jungle ponds are on fire inside me
I want to slice off my skin

burn gilt paper and pray for me

Cold—*Rengia*
Cricket—*Chungret*
Clock—*Condong*

I need to rest just a little more. Bopha, Vannith
obtain the elephants and oxen—

my dearest Annette, are you here?

I will name my most beautiful shell—*Pupina Mouhoti*
cannonballs are exploding in my head

where are we? my dear Abbe Hestrest
let me bring my lips to the divine cross
dangling from your neck

my piss is black
god-forsaken place

fill my glass again and we will toast
to the Wanderer who will walk with me

the Lord's prayer: *O Prea da cong lu mic*. . .

I'm freezing, I'm trembling
they are crying, my native boys

my dear man, more whiskey, more whiskey

my courageous Annette
I am tranquil
my journey has been sweet

mosquitoes plague me
the boy swats them

Give to—*Oi, chun*
Grief—*Chhu*
God—*Prea*

I want for nothing
At every halt, mandarins send me
elephants and provisions

my own, untie your hair . . .

ТНЄ ІNЋOCHINЄ CAPЄR

André Malraux and Clara Goldschmidt seek adventure in Indochina.

I

It was Paris. It was the twenties. Clara was a flapper, except her breasts were too bulky to be properly strapped down. André was a bon vivant, too skinny and self-conscious to achieve great success as a lady's man. She was avant-garde, an anarchist living on her family's fortune. It would be ten years before her husband would publish *Man's Fate* and be a celebrity; thirty years before he would become DeGaulle's secretary of cultural affairs and try to convince Mao to end the Vietnam War.

They were young. They both kept journals, but she hid hers, not sure he would approve. In their spare lodgings with a single Picasso on the wall they read anything they could get their hands on about Cambodia. Until their money ran out, they spent most nights drinking, conversing intensely with other bohemians. Breton, Satie, Chagall, Utrillo would also be there draped over sofas until morning's insipidness sent them all home.

André wouldn't dream of working for a living, so he concocted a scheme. They would go to Angkor, find some overlooked temples, pilfer some Buddhas and Shivas, and unload them in American museums. The perfect crime. The colonialists didn't care and the natives wouldn't stop them.

This was the life Clara always wanted, to make love underneath mosquito nets in seedy hotels with cranky ceiling fans, eat crepes filled with cinnamon-spiced mangoes cooked in the open air, and be carried in rickshaws by spindly-legged coolies. To prepare for the trip she bought quinine tablets, snakebite serum, a dozen hacksaws, and white linen for suits her mother's seamstress would sew.

II

In Siem Reap they arranged for a cook, a guide, oxcarts and drivers and bought three huge camphorwood chests. At daybreak they went off on horseback into the bush wearing cork helmets, cameras, compasses. Water bottles hung from their necks. Villagers using coupe-carts hacked a bullock trail to what was left of Banteay Srei Temple.

Clara and André tripped over broken flagstones, slipped on moss at the entrance to the courtyard. Vines and roots choked the pink sandstone fragments of bas-relief lying on the ground, but they wanted the intact frieze of multiple bare-breasted *apsaras*, divine chorus girls in an enchanted burlesque theater locked in four slabs on the temple walls.

It took three days . . . The couple offered to pay the locals more, but still they would not help. Their saws broke on the sandstone, sweat blinded them, mosquitoes brutalized them. They wrapped rags around their hands bleeding from crowbars and chisels, fighting exhaustion; the stones finally budged. They hoisted them on slings and slowly lowered them into camphorwood.

The *apsaras* are not smiling; their bejeweled ankles and wrists flail, because Vishnu and Brahma will not give the pirates leprosy, turn them into horned carabao doing the bidding of humans, or make Chitraratha's heavenly music pound cacophonously in their heads.

As much as the *apsaras* squirm and struggle, they are locked in the grip of sandstone and Indochine.

Note: André Malraux was sentenced to three years imprisonment and five years ban-ishment from Indochina for being in possession of statuary fragments obtained from an archaeological site. The charges against Clara Goldschmidt were dropped. On appeal Malraux was given a one-year suspended sentence. Silk Roads *by Alex Madsen (New York: Pharos Books, 1989) was used as a resource for this poem.*

THE HOTEL CAMBODIANA

It's always tea time at the Cambodiana.
We don't care about history here,
we own the manor.
We are the British in India,
the Italians in Eritrea,
the Dutch in Indonesia.
As far as we're concerned,
Cambodge will always be a French baguette.

If Cambodia were designed by Disney,
it would be the Cambodiana,
with orange-tiled pitched roofs and facades
turned up at the ends like leprechaun shoes,
where Khmer culture is an *apsara* with Barbie's body,
and stone Avalokitesvaras' smiling full-lipped mouths
adorn whiskey glasses.

We are too busy toasting ourselves
to hear the bulldozers flattening the huts
of the squatters outside the gate,
who come at the demolitionists with axes,
stupidly refusing to give up their land and
accept who they are:
never a well-stocked wine cellar,
always the olive in the bottom of a martini glass.

WHAT I KNOW

for Som Kim Ly

Why didn't the U.N. lady who interviewed me ask me what I know? If she opened up my skull, she would find big words in French and English wildly gesticulating at each other. The tourists who pay me to show them Angkor tell me I speak English better than they do, even the Americans who talk "real" English tell me so.

I'll bet the U.N. lady doesn't know the architectural terms I've memorized, like "laterite," "corbel arch," "pilaster," or while Europeans were burning everyone at the stake who didn't bow to their God, the Cambodian people were building cities to mirror the cosmology of Mount Meru, and our Buddha's emerald arms stretched from Vietnam westward to the Bay of Bengal and northward to Yunnan in China.

But to the U.N. lady, Cambodia is merely a latrine whose stench can be fumigated only by foreigners. I have no use for the words "democracy," "reconciliation," "party agent." No matter what Sihanouk now calls himself, he will always be a megalomaniac. All I know is that Pol Pot should have been plunged upside down into a barrel of water and drowned like the thousands he killed in Tuol Sleng. Instead, his murderous band will be legitimized in this election.

Someday I will be able to scrape up enough dollars to buy a bicycle and race at dusk to the Terrace of the Elephants built by the great Jayavarman VII. I will imagine the nobles cheering in the stands, as thick-skinned hulks stab each other with their ivory tusks. Then, before sleep, I will rub my hand across the bas-relief of the Sea of Churning Milk, where the Rakshasas and the good gods stopped their tug of war on Vasuki to extract the magic elixir *amrta*. Only one swallow and you won't die.

Even if she followed me in her four-wheel-drive vehicle into our glorious past, the U.N. lady would not drink, for her there is no *amrta*, only tap water where typhoid and dengue wrestle.

Picturing
Pol Pot

CHE PLACE WHERE DEACH LIVES

It took the Ohio National Guard thirteen seconds
to kill Jeffrey Miller, Allison Krause,
William Schroeder, and Sandra Scheuer.
They knew the war was spilling across the border,
but on May 4, 1970, they didn't know, we didn't know
about *Operation Breakfast*,
a B-52 strike against Base Area 353 inside Cambodia.
Ground controllers in Nam drank Coke
in their air-conditioned hootches counting down
the bombardiers—five, four, three, two, one—*hack*.
Long strings of bombs owned the sky,
throwing up geysers of earth, trees, and bodies.
It was only the beginning.
There would be a full menu of code names:
Lunch, Snack, Dinner, Dessert, Supper.

Maybe Allison who had joked with a guardsman
about a lilac appearing in the barrel of his M-I rifle
could imagine a man weighing yellow gold
in his village's open-air market
the split second before he is blown away,
or a woman weaving cloth
with silver thread for a wedding *sampot*,
the moment before she is ablaze,

but when we think of bombs,
they fall fast in hot wind
never arriving at the place where death lives.

*Note: The lines in the first stanza from "Ground controllers . . . Supper" are para-
phrased from* Sideshow: Kissinger, Nixon and the Destruction of Cambodia *by
William Shawcross (New York: Simon and Schuster, 1979), pages 23, 28. "Shortly
after noon on May 4, 1970, on a grassy knoll beyond Taylor and the Prentice Hall park-
ing lot, a contingent of Ohio National Guardsmen opened fire . . . striking thirteen . . . .
Four students were killed, one was permanently paralyzed and the others were wounded
in varying degrees of severity,"* A Gathering of Poets *by Maggie Anderson (Kent,
Ohio: Kent State University Press, 1991), page 1.*

OFF SCREEN

From 1966 until he was overthrown in 1970,
Prince Sihanouk produced nine feature films.

Sihanouk leaves political matters to others less inspired,
remaining behind a camera shooting
gold-sequined Royal ballet dancers,
their fingers bending backward.
In his Cambodia, he would never order
the severed heads of the rebellious carted
by the truckload to Phnom Penh.

The Prince gives the western world *Cambodge*, the film,
where his subjects alight from glistening Facel Vegas,
Cadillac convertibles, Jaguars, to glide into his palace,
swing to the squeal of his sax, and swill bubbly
from fluted glasses until dawn, and depart
imagining who will be chosen to bed him
when he retires to the royal chamber.

In his Cambodia, children do not die
with their joints on fire from dengue fever.
Skinny old men don't peddle *cyclos* up rutted roads,
their bones scraping taut leathered flesh,
until exhausted, they sleep in their cabs,
thin plastic covering against the rain's rage.

The movie mogul does not envision
clips of his young lovers kissing
in the backseats of chauffeur-driven Mercedes
being fed to Khmer Rouge rice-starved
adolescents like chocolates,
to spew forth a bile of jealousy and vindictiveness,
or that while he is under lock and key,
nineteen enemies of the revolution—
his children and grandchildren—
would be slaughtered off screen.

WITH A SMALL TYPEWRITER

*Found poem—extracted from the last message sent
by AP reporter Mean Leang, who was
killed in Phnom Penh on April 16, 1975.*

I alone in post office,
losing contact with our guys.
Only guy seeing me is Moonface at 1300.
I feel rather trembling.
Do not know how to file our stories.
Vichith lost his camera to the black-jacketed guys.
How quiet the streets.
Every minute changes.
I with a small typewriter
shuttle between the post office and home.
May be last cable today and forever.

PHNOM PENH AS STILL LIFE

The expulsion of the population from Phnom Penh is a measure one
will not encounter in any other country's revolution.
—Communist Party of Kampuchea document

They have even kicked us out of the hospitals.
Our bewildered loved ones carry intravenous bags
as we push them in their beds.
Weeping fathers hold our daughters
in bedsheet slings around their necks.
We hide rubies in the bottom of our cookpots
stuffed with sticky rice and green mangoes.
We carry our homes on our heads
or dangling from bamboo poles
and begin walking on wide roads
away from what we know.
We could be standing still
we walk so slowly.

In Phnom Penh geckos hide in the walls.
Offerings of lotus flower, mangosteen, and salak
waste on small home altars.
Gold leaf Buddha heads disappear
in the debris of *naga*-decorated *wats*.
Ravaged *cyclos*, their wheels and bicycle
seats pried off, lie on their sides.
Cold coal irons pine to glide
on white cotton again.
Hammocks tied between coconut palms
wait motionless for the bodies
they have caressed
to return . . .

EULOGY

Battambang, Cambodia, 1976

Forced to break my back in the rice paddies,
I longed to tell the heartless ones, kill me,
as I foraged sweet water algae and
water lily stalks for my moon-faced one,
hiding them in the *krama* I wrapped around my head.

But I will forever apologize to my lotus seed
for not smuggling out the crawlers to feed him.
Instead I crammed the raw crabs
we were forbidden to eat down my throat
as fast as I caught them.

Although I was as starved as those who did,
I couldn't bring myself to hack up the corpses
we found in the river or the forest,
but I brought my mango boy
manioc roots, marsh grass,
kapok sprouts, green locusts to roast
when I could sneak a fire.

His tiny belly was too bloated,
his fingernails black.
Cramps rocked his body.
Water leaked out of his anus.
I had to fool the heartless ones.
I covered his face
with my red and white checked *krama*.
Approaching with their rice buckets
they thought I was shading my little rambutan
while he slept.
The ruse worked.
My other children opened their mouths
and with their grey tongues
swilled in extra grains of plump watery rice.

PICTURING POL POT

for Vann Nath

They do not execute me
because I will paint Pol Pot's picture.
They let me sleep in a room
with other painters and sculptors.
We stop starving and
no longer wear leg irons.
I scrutinize His black and white photograph
looking for the evil.
They give me charcoal.
My picture is to look just like the photograph,
but I need colors to give a portrait life.
When I use color and water
they are happy with me.

I paint Him plump and benign,
but in my mind
he is Ravana, the demon king
with twenty fisted hands severed at the wrist
and ten heads that once spewed fire
licked clean to their skulls by rats.

He is a giant scream of an infant
who messed himself and has to wait
for me to clean him up.

He is a mosquito tired of flailing
who landed in the ceramic rainwater barrel
next to my house just in time
for the wooden lid to slam in place
and kill the sky.

*Note: Vann Nath survived Tuol Sleng. He escaped in 1979
when Vietnamese troops entered Phnom Penh. In that same
year he was painting scenes of prison life at the new Tuol
Sleng Genocide Museum.*

CHE INCERROGACION

You are in a tiny cell of bricks.
They chain your feet together,
burn the soles with cigarettes.
You think it is the afternoon.

You want to give the sublime confession,
the one that will save your life.

The first time you say you are a loyal cadre.
You tried to poison your husband's rice
when he muttered in his sleep, "CIA,"
but that is the wrong answer.

The next time they sew the soles of your bleeding feet
with black thread and say, *You swine, confess*.
You wipe your face along the mud floor.
Say you hoarded medicines.
Beg to be forgiven for your selfishness.
Still the wrong answer.

The last time they smash your bleeding head
into red bricks—you spit blood
and say

*Note: During Pol Pot's reign of terror, Tuol Sleng or Security Office
21 was an extermination center in Phnom Penh, primarily for high-
ranking cadre. Of the seventeen thousand people processed there, only
seven survived, "A Journey Through Genocide" by John Pilger, The
Guardian, January 29, 2004.*

POL POT'S WIFE TALKS
TO WHOEVER WILL LISTEN

Khieu Ponnary is going mad in the
service of her husband's revolution.
—Elizabeth Becker

I

Before the corpses,
Sar kissed my fingertips
and clung to my every word
as if they had wings
and could fly him to a black pajama Utopia.

In Keng Vannsak's apartment
on Rue du Commerce
I flirted with Sar in French.
I knew everything:
Stalin's tract "On The National Question,"
Lenin's "On Imperialism."
Talking revolution was sexy.
I would brush against Sar's shoulder
and whisper "Destroy the bourgeoisie,
re-educate the masses."

II

Before, I pretended words were white
lotus flowers in cloisonne vases,
declawed cats, or impotent men,
but they have always been murderous.

Pol Pot locked me in this house.
Sar would never allow this.
He will come and stroke my hair and
tell me no one is dying,

but the corpses won't let me sleep.
They curse me, press into me—
inseminate me with their agony.

My words want to wear grey pinafores
as I did in the French Lycee,
but can only don black—
the color of the world.

*Note: Keng Vannsak moved to Paris in 1946. He
was an ardent nationalist with anti-royalist lean-
ings and influenced Pol Pot's politics.*

NOT A PERSONA POEM

*Nhem Ein was the Khmer Rouge
photographer at Tuol Sleng.*

Your mother died when you were two.
I don't care
why your father,
a poor bean farmer,
gave you away to the Khmer Rouge.
I refuse to climb into your head
as I have with so many others.
I will not say "I" when I mean "you."

If I get in spitting distance of you,
in the museum you knew
as a death camp, watch out.

You think you are so special.
No training in hurling grenades for you.
Instead, they send you to Shanghai
to learn the art of light
and by sixteen you are a big shot,
the Chief Photographer of Tuol Sleng.

I won't "be" you,
you who want memory to be a darkroom
where chemicals make
the mutilated disappear.
You hide behind your camera,
but I won't hide with you.
In my dreams my father cradles
his weak heart like a puppy,
but in your nightmares
passive faces are always pleading.

The ten thousand "traitors"
you saw through your viewfinder
wore reuseable number tags.
They knew the click of your Leica
was the sound
before the world explodes.

ELECTRIC CAN OPENER

*Ophthalmologists in Long Beach, California,
have noticed a disturbingly high incidence of vision
problems among Little Phnom Penh's female refugees.*

The doctors for eyes say that their newest,
most expensive machines show my eyes can see,
so why do I know the gold-plated Buddha
in the corner of the living room only
by its hard metallic curves or recognize
the racy durian by its prickly
armor and nauseating stench?
When I chew the betel nut
I don't care what the Americans think
of my black teeth. I don't care if I trip
on the back steps after beating
the rug on the line and seeing
our old hut on stilts
at the edge of the Tonle Sap,
our underwater bamboo box
swelling with fish twitching and jerking.

I have memorized where each object in the kitchen stays.
We couldn't be bothered with gadgets
before we moved here.
I trap a can of baby corn under the blade
until it's caught in the teeth, and listen
to the racket as it spins and cuts
into the flimsy tin, when again—
a ferocious bonfire and I am back
in the circle watching
the Angka club my friends,
pick them up by arms and legs and hurl them
onto the pyre yelping and shrieking.

The Librarian

He cannot stop thinking about Pol Pot's cadre
living inside the French antebellum yellow building
of the National Library in Phnom Penh,
where book corpses shared the grounds with pigs
and human swine wrenched books off shelves,
yanked out pages of palm and mulberry leaves
to light fires or roll their own smokes.

He knows there are more books
in his small branch library in Brooklyn
than in all of Cambodia in 1977.

He dutifully dusts the dust jackets of all the books,
but they do not mind and snap to attention
when he claps his hands.
He cannot make the *Cliff Notes* patrons disappear,
nor stop the library from subscribing to *Reader's Digest*,
so he must on his own time edit out the
histories of horrors pummeled into paragraphs.
At least on the pages that his palms caress
bombs will become bowling balls.

If only he could polish each phrase,
thaw every frozen syllable, wouldn't the healing begin?
                                    Doesn't ink soak up blood?

ON THE ROAD WITH ST. PAUL

Kang Kek Ieu, alias Duch, headed National
Security for the Khmer Rouge in Tuol Sleng.

Christ Jesus came into the world to save
sinners, of whom I am the chief.
Timothy I:15

The man who wrote, *Use the hot method*
even if it kills him, says he met Saul on the road,

and out of nowhere: a blinding light,
a chill wind, the sound of a roaring sea and
a voice beseeching, *Why do you persecute me?*

When he stayed at Saul's place,
the inn on Straight Street,
blindness fell from his eyes like scales.

Now Duch prays for Jesus' forgiveness,

solicits funds for Christian textbooks and
waits in a small hut in Cambodia with his son
who stepped on a landmine
and wears a wooden leg with carved toes.

Note: Duch has been imprisoned in Phnom Penh since 2000.

ELEGY

On April 18, 1998, Pol Pot was cremated.

I

Long ago as the Buddha sat under the Tree
attaining supreme knowledge,
Mara the Evil One feared his subjects
would revolt and betray him.
So the Evil One brought forth his army
of soldiers with pig ears and bodies like jugs
to crumple the sun and moon.
Mara's rains submerged cities and shook mountains,
but his weapons fell to the ground as flowers,
while the Serene One remained cross-legged,

so we in our sacks of skin,
crossing and uncrossing our legs,
could still seek him.

II

Today, the day Pol Pot's body will be set on fire,
we eat rice as usual.
In mud underneath our stilt huts piglets suckle.
We wash our black hair outside in rainwater,
but we want something miraculous:
the end of evil,
when everyone he killed
and we loved
will return to us.

III

His corpse, preserved with chunks of ice,
is lifted from a narrow bed
and lowered into a crude wooden coffin.
Crammed in with him is his straw fan,
red and white checked *krama*,
and a small black knapsack with his clothes.
The pyre is made of his mattress
with old tires underneath,

and upside down
on top of the coffin
the wicker chair he liked to sit in.

A plastic cigarette lighter sets it ablaze.

Flames wrap around his blackened skeleton,
its right fist raised.

His wife and daughter are not there.
Perhaps the Buddha is,
bestowing sprays of white and pink fuchsia.

Note: In Section III several lines are paraphrased from
"Pol Pot Cremated; No Tears Shed" by Seth Mydans,
New York Times, *April 19, 1998.*

Absentee Ballot

KHMER ADVICE ON PROTECTION FROM MINES

1. Do not play with mines.

2. Do not go near mines.

3. Do not touch or pick up things that are unknown.

4. Do not touch valuable things in unlikely places.

5. Do not go to unknown or prohibited places.

6. Watch out for booby trapped items in areas where fighting is ongoing.

7. Do not go into areas that are likely to be mined areas or people say are mined.

8. Follow in the footsteps of the person in front if possible.

9. Pray to ancestors, wear amulets, and apply tattoos.

10. Have a strong belief in the power of magic and the magical powers of the person who provides this protection.

11. Always ask villagers what places are mined. Most of the time they know the exact places where mines have been laid.

12. Assume that there is more than one mine and that mines have been planted in groups.

13. Mark the mine using a marking sign.

Note: Distributed at a briefing for new U.N. volunteers, SNC, Phnom Penh, July 1992.

THE REAPER

In Cambodia, landmines kill or maim three hundred people each month.
One mine remains in the ground for every two people in the country.

He is not in Kurdistan, Somalia, Angola,
Afghanistan, or Kuwait, but Cambodia.
The Khmers know him as another white foreigner
telling them he is better at what
they have been forced to learn to do,
but they are sure that this expert
with the expensive equipment
will save at least one life, maybe more,
planting in reverse.
He is the blind walking gingerly with a metal detector
and a stick praying for weightlessness,
plucking out death melons,
innocent paddies swallowed with rice seeds.

The villagers follow him, even the one riding a bicycle
with his remaining hand and leg.
They want to show him how they marked
where the death potatoes hide.
Over here, underneath the tree stump painted red.
There, beneath a bundle of upright sticks tied together with grass.
Behind you, below a plastic bag tied to a bamboo branch.

They must lead him
to the black buds
before they shriek into blossom.

ᴄhᴇ ᴇᴠᴀᴄᴜᴀᴛɪᴏɴ

Sihanoukville, Cambodia's seaside paradise, nestles in the translucent
waters of the Gulf of Siam. One can appreciate cool breezes supplemented
by sparkling clear skies, while butterflies paint the shores.
—Cambodian Tourist Bureau

Frightened throngs packed into buses, taxis and a train today, fleeing [Siha-
noukville] . . . where a vast mound of possibly toxic waste was discovered.
—*New York Times,* December 22, 1998

Sopheap, we have to get out of here,
dress the children,
take the family pictures from the altar.

(all killed when Pol Pot poisoned us)

The Taiwanese ship brought evil.
Bopha, Mok's cousin who cleaned out its hold,
too weak except to crawl,
was found dead,

(blotched and bloated,
his mouth wide open,
as if to gulp air)

your gold bangles,
nothing else.

I know you told me not to be such a busybody,
but while you were buying rice and lotus flowers
I went to the dump to see
if the white plastic bags would be good for storing rice.
When I pierced them, clumps of cement
and dirt spilled out.

(the earth holds my brutality too—
beige plastic papaya-shaped containers
with thousands of black exploding seeds.
I will never forget where they hide)

You think I'm stupid!
As soon as I got home,
I scrubbed my hands raw.

(right now, because of me, someone
could be screaming—
a white-shirted student on his moped
coming home from English class,
his stomach shredding,
his intestines spilling out;
a rice farmer stepping into
his green skim pond,
his foot severing . . .)

Sopheap, they say Khim Bo took bribes
so Taiwan can waste us
and spare their own.

(I haven't slept in days,
even in the hammock
I won't close my eyes, afraid
to see lepers
their fingers wasted away

my feces are water)

Sopheap, don't worry about the pigs or the chickens.
For a few days they will stay
under the house bewildered,
but then will go wild.

I heard in America by a canal trees turned black,
slime burned holes in children's shoes,
and in Japan bones grew soft,
children were born strange,
Sopheap, hands coming directly out of shoulders.

Sopheap, I said take nothing else!

A CARTOGRAPHER'S VIEW
OF THE WORLD

I make the map that magically unfolds in your lap,
the plastic globe that bobs on your palm
like a buoy in the Indian Ocean
to tell you how small your world is.
I feel at peace when I can scale down 1,000,000 centimeters
of fir trees in Ratanakiri *khaet*, Cambodia,
to = 1 centimeter and hold back the great waters of the Tonle Sap
beneath my pointer and ring finger.

That Roman crackpot Gaius Julius Solinus made marks on paper
to symbolize mountains and woodlands like I do,
but that is where we part company;
his speciality was to fabricate the unknown.
I want to plop Uzbekistan into your living room and show you
how it rubs elbows with Afghanistan. In his Asia
horsefooted men had earlobes so long
they covered their entire bodies, and webbed hands so large
they doubled as parasols against the blinding sun.

But when I am up in the U.N. chopper in Kratie *khaet*
taking aerial shots of its *sroks, khums, phuums,*
it could be 1939 and I am sitting next to Virgil Kauffman,
the father of aerial photogrammetry;
when he stops the engine for an instant
in his open cockpit
my arms and camera tilt out so far
I capture the images unblurred and pure.

My job is to expose what is, not what was.
There are other people paid to dig up the past.
In Saknoy commune I locate three villages
San Knuoy, Sre Tapan, Hang Savat.
The villages no longer there do not interest me.
I won't listen to their dead.
I will not hear you or the chanting
from the rubble of phantom pagodas.
I refuse to limn what I cannot see.

PROSCHESIS MAKER

I guess I'm lucky
to still have one leg
and a job where I can play like the gods
making legs of wood, leather, and old tires
for those of us whose karma
is to step on small containers of evil.

I have a lot of time to think
molding calves, kneecaps, ankles, heels.

Because there are so many of us limbless ones,
maybe in two or three generations,
mothers will give birth to one-handed
one-legged babies.
Then no one will assume
I am a beggar
built not to be loved.

One night I'll come back to the workshop late
after getting drunk watching the racing boats
at the Omtuk Festival to find
all the pathetic imitations
have become real, brown and fleshy
with splayed toes that will soon know
the goosh of wet earth and will run
outside and fling themselves
back into the family of the body.

SUMMER OF THE SECRET BALLOT

Phnom Penh, 1992

We are constructing a house of registration cards
that will withstand the wolf of tyranny.
In these light-filled rooms
you can choose who will speak for you,
and not be bribed with rice
or have your daughter threatened.

We do not want to know
what is happening in Bosnia—
men forced to castrate their friends and
drill holes in other men's chests,
children impaled on spikes,
young women gang raped,
impregnated by the seed of the enemy.

We are replacing horror with registration sites.
If your grandmother was born in Cambodia,
you can sit with democracy on an old school bench
and wait to have your photo I.D. taken
in front of a white sheet
with liberty stitched into the fabric.
You can feel equality in the sticky gel
that will develop your picture,
and justice in your thumb
made ready to press its glorious print
into the thick paper of your own
soon to be plastic-coated card of hope.

THE BAT COLLECTION

The statues are alright as long as we sweep.
Khun Samet—Cambodia National Museum

We must welcome these night creatures
who lounge and titter under our leaky roof
and splitting eaves, and shit
on the false ceiling and statues below.
Our pay checks are always late,
if we get paid at all,
but their guano is excellent
commanding eighteen cents
per pound at the market.

As they devour insects and
their voices echo, we fill our noses
with sandalwood incense and jasmine.
Dawn and noon we gather guano.

Their gift is our obsession.
We scrub and scrape
the flecks of their stinky contribution
from sandstone and bronze surfaces,
off coiled *nagas* and Garuda's wings,
Durga's flowing garment,
busts of the once four-handed Vishnu
and the armless statues
of the great Jayavarman VII
who, mercifully, will never know
what happened to his Angkor.

POEM TO THOM'S WIFE

While he was with me in Saigon,
haggling with street venders
over the authenticity of Zippo lighters
with phrases like ONLY THE HEADS SURVIVE
and LET ME WIN YOUR HEART AND MIND
OR I'LL BURN YOUR GOD DAMN HUT DOWN
etched into the metal,

were you conjuring him
showering your face with kisses
after he unwrapped the windsurfer figurine
you gave him last year for Christmas?

You refuse to imagine me,
but I see you
on his Harley, wedged against his back,
your arms tight around his waist,
flying down the backroads of Texel Island.

To excuse myself for betraying you
I make you unworthy
of his love, ordinary, boring—
pulling your fat son away from computer games,
as I change the course of Cambodian history.

What are you doing right now?

Your husband and I are sitting
on my porch watching a procession.
He is holding my hand.
Khmers are carrying platters piled high
with passion fruits for the engaged couple next door.

Are you picking out his birthday card?
Are you putting candles in the windows for when he returns?
Is the ruby ring he sent you too tight?

ON THE SISOPHON EXPRESS

By March 1993, 340,000 Cambodian refugees
were repatriated from Thai border camps.

I love where I am.
On this train.
Not back with the orphans
or arriving
at a place more lonely
than the long open hut—
no room between my bed
and the kid who also has nobody.

On my lap is a cardboard box.
Inside, a small mirror,
a toothbrush missing bristles,
the string pants and T-shirt
I wash to wear the next day,
and the mallets for playing the *rameat thung*.
My wrists are still limber.
Soon I will stroke bamboo keys again.

I do not push to look out the window.
I remember:
panting carabaos yoked together and
the unquenched thirst of rice paddies.
Underneath my feet is the rice ration
supposed to last forty days.

I had to choose:
land or $50. I hide the money
where no one will steal it.
There is no land without my family.
If they are alive
they will find me.

Before I left the camp my teacher gave me
his precious wooden mallets and said,
Here are my thin-stemmed lotus flowers.
Go . . . find my teacher.

ABSENTEE BALLOT

Monkol Won Registration Site, November 5, 1992

The musicians are not here today to distract you
by practicing on brass-nippled containers housed in semicircles
inside the room next to the registration site. To get away
from election talk you must walk past the young cripple
who crawls everyday on his gnarled legs to the benches to unfurl
his book of color postcards of the life of the Buddha,
past the old woman vendor who will sell you one cigarette, past
the still young girl hawking plums soaked in sugar and rice wine,
to your spot behind the shacks of the Donchee, where you will squat,
your underpants around your knees, for a quiet pee.
The sun is sticking to your body and you want to speak English directly,
not through an interpreter. You are exhausted from bawling out
the Ghanaian Civ Pol who sat on his ass instead of
helping to transport a bunch of Buddhist monks
who stood in their saffron robes against our white sheet backdrop
giving us the honor of photographing them for their voter I.D. cards.

You are tired of pretending to be the authority on democracy,
when you believe all governments stink,
some just smell more rank than others.
As you sing the praises of the secret ballot, you pray
that no one will step on newly laid land mines walking to the polling site.
You have to make sure that the registrars know
not to let the laminator overheat and to roll the fleshy part
of the thumb firmly over the ink pad to catch the whorls.

You have to play by the rules and allow the Khmer elder
who came all the way from Canada to exercise his right to vote,
but not his wife, because although she "is" Cambodian,
she was raised in Kampuchea Krum, a chunk of Cambodia bitten off
by Vietnam before she was born. You have to learn to deal
with the obnoxious party agents of the **BLDP** and **FUNCINPEC**
who try to exclude the Vietnamese from registering
because they blame the Yuons for destroying the country,
but excuse the Khmer Rouge as merely the black sheep of the family.
As you slowly pull up your underpants, you remember
the absentee ballot in your pocket that you received too late
to clink your two cents into the election box back home,
where you felt your vote was a message in a bottle never found.

ACCIDENT ON ACHAR MEAN

When you walk on Achar Mean
you do not think "lotus flower,"
recognize bodhisattvas or trip over the green-faced Rama.
Boys hawk yellow and blue feather dusters and
tattered bootlegged copies of English travel guides
with Angkor Wat's five conical towers
smack on the covers,
while wall-eyed widows who once had legs
grab at you as you pass.

But today you are not on foot;
you are above the riffraff
in the driver's seat of
a U.N. vehicle buffed white,
the color Cambodians wear for funerals.

Toy brown young men
wearing synthetic short-sleeved shirts
race next to you
on tiny red mopeds,
as scrawny, dried string-bean men
slowly pedal doll families home and
steer clear of you.

But one *cyclo* driver does not scurry.
You nick his puny wheels
and drag him under the chassis.
You slam on the brakes.
When he crawls out
he is bleeding.

You climb down and
scrounge around for *luy*,
finding about twenty bucks
in your pockets.

The *cyclo* driver bows and backs away facing you.
His fingertips touch the tip of his nose
and tightly pressed between his palms
is his fortune.

THE WHITE WHIRLYBIRD WITH THE
BLACK LETTERS MAKES A LANDING

Stung, Kampong Thom, Cambodia

The copter with the massive "UN" on its sides and bottom circles the clearing. Brown children with shiny hair the color of licorice run to the vision miraculous as Pushpaka, the chariot that raced through the sky carrying Ravana the demon king. The children found this marvelous machine once before in a bootlegged Schwarzenegger movie. They know it will never belong to their parents, but to rich white people who are supposed to help them. They hold their *kramas* to their faces against the dust kicked up by the helicopter's fake wind. They wait for the loud noise to stop, hoping to be allowed to touch the body, sleek as lily pads, and the propellers whose spinnings hold the secret of flight. Some become bold when the people don't come out. They start crawling on the sides of the helicopter, while others pick up pebbles and start pelting the metal. But then the people climb down. There are five of them. Four men and one woman. The children are surprised that one has skin darker than their own and that the woman is small like their mothers, but very old, because she has grey hair. The most important one, wearing a blue beret, a green uniform, and high black boots, isn't smiling. He picks up a pile of pebbles and slowly lets them spill from his palm. They guess he is trying to tell them to stop the pelting. Some of them take this as a chance to amplify their attack and get into it with new vigor, causing all the people except the important one to duck and run inside the marvelous machine. The important one is yelling guttural sounds in his strange language. Although the children know he is angry, they are having too good a time to stop, until the propellers start whipping up dust and they are forced to cease playing. They look up. The aircraft is so far away it is Ravana's chariot gliding over the Dangrek Mountains. Except the mountains are now bald. The forests sold to Thailand for coffee tables.

COUNSELING IN PHNOM PENH

Patrick Griffin from Bray, County Wicklow, doesn't care a whit
about Yeats or Synge or Behan, and was certain
there was not a basement in all of Ireland
needing cement poured or a pathway requiring gravel.
He was tired of sitting on his arse and knew working for UNTAC,
even as a volunteer, would make him more money
than on the dole. His sympathies lay with the IRA.
He got off on the idea of inventorying Polaroid cameras,
laminating machines, and the thin plastic-covered
registration cards, giving Khmers the right to vote in their first
"real" election in the land of skulls and minefields.

Maybe with a change of scene he would stop boozing.
But he arrived in Cambodia shit-faced and could not stop,
because Tiger Beer was dirt cheap and weed was sold in the market
like fucking lettuce, and Khmer cops frequented the opium dens
not to pummel, but to partake. Maybe in a place where nobody knew him
he would finally get Mary Gillie, her cheating self, out of his system.
In her patent leather pocketbook he would find men's phone numbers.
Later in bed, when he would touch her, she would feign sleep.

After a row with his landlord during his last drinking bout,
the U.N. said: *counseling or repatriation*, so he decided
to see the lady shrink. Patrick didn't think it would bother her
if he brought along Sopheap, his girl, who he met at a disco
with the same strobe lights freezing you in space
as when the Americans bombed Cambodia.
Sopheap came back to his room and never left.
He gave her money to buy *numpan* and toothpaste and a little extra
for high heels and 501 imitation jeans at the Psaa Tmay.

The shrink knew Patrick was not alone because she heard Sopheap
scream as they stepped over a dead rat on the landing.
Since she spoke only rudimentary Khmer
the shrink told him she couldn't do couple counseling.
He said that wasn't what he had in mind.
He just wanted Sopheap near him.
As she wedged herself into the side of his body,
Patrick Duffin talked about finding his mother on the parlour floor
after she had mixed herself a shandy of Valium and Guiness.

CHEIR ROOM

Thom had no wife, no children in their room late at night
while they listened to the click click clackclickclack clack
of the noodle seller's stick against bamboo.

Sometimes she would think of oxbowed animals
motionless in flooded mercury-colored fields,
as his razor culled her black curls,
leaving her mons a blank slate;
soon their bodies would become
the Tonle Sap running backward.

CHINESE NEW YEAR

Phnom Penh, 1993

Earlier that night the soldier lying with her
underneath the mosquito net had tied one on
with an American-Chinese Khmer contractor who came back
to scoop up some real estate and take advantage
of the cheap labor, but says he will haul his butt out
before the Elections, since the Khmer Rouge have changed in name only
and that this democracy charade is nothing more
than a minefield waiting for a jeep or a bare foot.

When she's not sure if the boom boom boom below her balcony
is mortar shells or flares and squibs set off by local kids,
she will wake her soldier and he will slur, *I'm here. Don't worry.*
or rant about how the American Khmer kept filling
his glass and spitting, *They're not ready for freedom.*
All they know is nepotism and the value of gold and
then how he told the sell-out to fuck-off.
Why am I here making it safe for free and fair elections,
when you're fucking your own people?

When he is too nauseous to sleep, he will lean over the toilet
and keep saying, *Where is Elana?*
You're not Elana. You're her sister.
She will hold back tears and repeat, *Thom, it's me, it's me.*
I have no sister.

Elana will let this man become Cambodia,
the elections merely a backdrop to their bodies—
firecrackers imploding together night after night after night.

After the mission he will return to his wife
and send letters that close with, *I will always love you.*
Smelling of vomit and whiskey, tonight he is not her net,
tossing her to the moon and catching her in the weft of his body.
As the Year of the Rooster crows, 14-year-old DK boys with assault rifles
fire on Vietnamese fisherfolk, until they stop flapping.

MOTOROLA: IN MEMORIAM

Although you always slept with me,
I have forgotten the feel of your black body,
of your face, if your channel window was round
or square, your antenna rubbery or hard.
But I remember how you snored standing up,
how I snapped on the belt clip prepping you for morning.
I can still hear you squeal when your batteries were depleted.
I want to hold you close to my mouth and whisper,
Come in, Over—Come in, Over.

But no one is listening.
Today I strain to remember all the voices inside you
with handles like *Romeo Bravo, Echo Charlie Seven, Omega Mike One,*
who spoke in the official language of the world: English,
but whose accents held their homelands—
Pakistan, Bulgaria, the Netherlands, Indonesia.

Sometimes after work Cambodians turned subversive
and talked into you in their own language,
telling friends they had to stop
to fill up their *motos* with petrol,
before arriving with mangoes and Marlboros,
until the walkie-talkie police broke in and told them to *Knock it off.*

No one is answering to *Echo Charlie* now
or listening to the moment on Election Day, May 1993,
when the Olympic Stadium gates were thrown open,
voters clamored over the chain link fence to be the first in line,
and my voice trumpeted through the tough plastic:
We actually pulled it off!

Note: Ninety-seven percent of Khmers registered to vote actually voted in the first "free and fair" election since French colonialization.

The Vow

SWEET-TALKING GUY

He is lying on a rented straw mat
listening to the slap of the waves at Parangtritis Beach
with a woman who could have children his age.
Tonight he does not have to sweet talk
outside a trinket shop in Yogya.

He tells the woman who will bankroll him to Bali:
On this spot the Queen of the South Seas shed
her glittering scales and crawled
to embrace her beloved Sultan of Solo.

Tomorrow morning he will be a virgin—
his first passage on a ferry
over the strait to Bali;
he will blush in his new bathing suit
no self-respecting Javanese
would consent to wear,
and he will spit out the strange ice cream,
its cold sweetness stinging.

But now under the night sky with no moon
he conjures Bali for the woman:
Our bed will face a tropical forest
where macaque snatch bananas from your hands
and I will tuck red hibiscus behind your ears.

UNSENT LETTER TO SUNARSO

Sept. 20, 1999

I fear you have become
one of the staggering young men
you once ridiculed,
who fall down in the Square laughing
as their wondrous blood oozes
onto the pavement.

Do you still read to the old people
who have forgotten how to suffer?
Does the nurse still slip you
that little cocktail of something and
voila! you believe you are the greatest
dalang ever to breathe
life into shadow puppets
who throb from your touch,
moan in your voice,
feign love with your ardor.

Do husbands on your side of the screen
still pray that the small wooden wand
between the first two toes of your right foot
won't hit the *kechrek's* metal plates perfectly
and that their wives on the shadow side
will not be lost in your thunder?

I haven't been anywhere exotic
since I knew you, except Tahiti,
where prostitutes dress as women
and travelers eat thin pancakes
slathered with chocolate
by a river lit with tiny white lights.

I still talk deeply to younger men,
but in my office they pay for my wisdom.
We do not touch.
Each one arrives by appointment,
sits on my small couch, and
I, on the longer.
Like you, they all want to leave home,
be magnificent, and love women
they will never marry.

I LOOK IN MY PASSPORT AT THE TRIANGLE STAMPED 27 FEB 1993

when I thought
I would never see you again.

Without you, I occupied myself
with a person no more than a shadow
puppet and a tinkle of bells,
as you sprawled in the recliner of your wife.

After two weeks wrenched apart;
a lifetime then,
you find me
in a cheap hotel
off Bangkok's Patpong Road,
where it is always nighttime.
Outside our window
a boy's nipples are being pinched
by a potential customer.

I finally let myself fall into sleep
with my head
in the small of your back as before,
lulled into a country never found
in a passport.

LOVE LETTERS

He writes that his hard dick misses her mouth
and he prays she isn't a butterfly any longer
flittering from *farang* to *farang*,
taking other men to their old hotel;

he doesn't write that his wife's huge breasts
cause her back to ache and if he
isn't too tired at night he presses his hands
between her shoulder blades to ease the pain,

only apologizes for not sending money,
saying he is saving every penny to return to Bangkok
to feed his doll *khow pat moo*, pork fried rice,
at that little hole in the wall and wipe the grease off her chin;

he doesn't say he keeps machines rolling at a commercial laundry
where pressed sheets and pillow cases are yanked off
conveyor belts by Vietnamese, Cambodian, Chicano girls
no older than she, or that his wife can't work,
believing that when she leaves the house her heart will explode;

he tells his cuddlee wuddlee to learn English,
not to pay a translator to read his letters, not to make fuck
with *farangs* who won't wear condoms;

he doesn't mention the brown kinky-haired women
who get into his beat-up car and press their faces to his groin,
or the images of Oriental girls waiting for him inside his computer;

he says he can drive anything from a tractor to a limo,
so why couldn't he sprint around her town
in a little three-wheeled *tuk-tuk* overcharging tourists,
and turn her into an honest woman—
giving her a life she couldn't possibly imagine.

FOR MYO MYO: HORSECART DRIVER #142

Bagan, Myanmar, 1993

She doesn't know why Myo Myo who hauls foreigners
to see Pagan, its name and glory erased
by Ne Win who rules based on what his astrologers
declare unlucky, got her on the bus
off limits to a rucksacked tourist with a *Lonely Planet* guidebook,
since government greed has made it criminal not to fly.
Maybe he wanted to be subversive without dying for it.
Maybe he was still enraged at a government
who gave him a week to clear out of his hometown.
Perhaps he hoped she would contribute
in dollars toward the house he builds in his mind
on the banks of the Irrawaddy River.

Burmese women passengers wearing *longyis* and
paste on their faces from the bark of acacia trees
peek at her when they think she is sleeping
or when her head is down, as she digs dirt
out of her nails with a tiny knife.
They all go into a café for the umpteenth time
for a fix of thick coffee with
long strings of condensed milk in cracked cups,
as the bus mechanic yanks something that looks like
a ginseng root out of the engine,
so the old vehicle can continue to stagger along through the night.
For twelve dollars in kyats,
seated in a place of honor behind the monks,
she is on her way to Yangoon and home.

Note: Until 1990, when the Burmese government forcibly moved Pagan village and relocated its residents, villagers lived in a small settlement inside the old city walls of the great civilization of Pagan. It is believed that villagers were relocated because they supported Aung San Suu Kyi's democracy movement.

LOVE POEM

*Aung San Suu Kyi has been under detention
in one form or another for the last seventeen
years. Her husband Michael Aris died
March 27, 1999, of prostate cancer.
He was denied a final visit to his wife.*

While meditating I think
how are our sons holding up.
The thought becomes smoke…
When my gaze is soft
and a mosquito nips me,
I don't flick it off.

But you understood
before we married
that I would not allow the junta
to kill my country,
even if they took you away from me.

I was so grateful for the Nordic Trak
and the sheet music,
especially during the time they let only
young Thwin look in on me.

I do not need to touch the piano
to hear *The French Suites'* sarabande.
I played it endlessly,
until strings snapped, keys stuck
and I was reduced to picking
"Twinkle, Twinkle Little Star . . . "

The last time they allowed you to visit
we sat on the hard piano bench,
your thigh against mine;
I attempted to play a Bach gigue,
when joy swept us up,
and we leapt higher and higher,
the wooden floor our trampoline;
the room spinning—
I flung myself into your arms.

JOHNNY GOT HIS GUN

*Karen rebel leaders Luther and Johnny Htoo led the
"God's Army" in Burma. On January 24, 2000, ten members
of the group took over a hospital in Ratchaburi, Thailand.
Luther and Johnny and other "God's Army" followers
have since surrendered to Thai Police.*

You want to see my guns?
I have M-16s and AK-47s and grenade launchers.
You want to watch me shoot a weapon?
It would be fun, but I better not.
Burmese army could hear.

250,000 invisible soldiers are under my command.
My twin brother Johnny commands a mere 150,000,
but he can change form,
while I stay twelve years old
with a "Love" tattoo on my arm
and a cheroot in my mouth.

One day Johnny was washing himself in a stream
when he called out, *Look at me.*
He became an old man with white hair and a long beard.
Then jumped back into the water
and was twelve again.

Grown-ups follow us because they believe
we have a direct line on heaven.
They think we are incarnates
of great leaders who fell in battle.

If I decide I want to kill
twenty people today,
all I have to do is point my rifle down.
Twenty bullets lodge in the dirt and
twenty enemies are dead somewhere.

We don't stay anywhere very long,
but I like my life,
except when my visible soldiers
start singing hymns.
I really try to listen.
I even sing a word or two,
but I yawn too much anyway.
Smoking a cheroot helps.
Crawling into the lap of one of the old guys
really, really helps.

Give me your tape recorder.
I want to press the buttons and hear my voice.
No, I'd rather have a piggy-back ride.
Lift me up.

Note: "Johnny Got His Gun" contains a quote by Johnny
Htoo, recalled by his brother; several lines are paraphrased
from "Burmese Rebel Chief More Boy Than Warrior," by
Seth Mydans, New York Times, April 9, 2000.

ODE TO A BETEL CHEW

Once you made the rice grow faster,
the sleeping mat thicker,
the husband less sour—
now I want only you.

Before I married,
in my father's garden
green areca nuts poked out in wild clusters
below palm fronds of lanky trees,
as glossy broad betel leaves
shimmied up kapok trees.

Now the sea is too far
to find snails in wet sand
to burn and crush with a hammer
for a lime paste coat on the
plump betel leaf's pale green underside.

Although I have a small quid of you
in my cheek, I need more.
At the market I'll haggle a good price
for nuts just relieved from the palm
and leaves piled high
as bolts of batik in a stall.

Then, I will refill my bamboo lime container,
so I can chew you with my beautiful black teeth
and feel your blood fill my mouth.

LEARNING TO SUFFER

She will never tell Thom the story
of locks shorn for love of dharma,
because today she is traveling
through Mandalay alone.

In Burma when a boy becomes a monk
he is dressed in clothes stitched with tiny mirrors;
his lips are painted red,
and he mounts an elephant.
Like Siddhartha, he is learning to suffer.
Before the boy dons the magenta robe,
he visits a barber in his lean-to with posters
of Thai movie stars on the palm frond walls,
to rid himself of vanity.
The barber cuts and shaves the scalp
until his skull looks like the moon.

The room in the Taiseng Hotel
on Achar Mean is no longer theirs.
Maybe a Civpol from Algeria hired to set up roadblocks
was performing absolution in their room,
or a Malay businessman from Singapore
who opened a fax store and had a different
Vietnamese whore every night
was throwing his tie on the bureau
where Jayavarman VII's head had been,
on top of the old *sout* remnant
Khmers say silkworms
no longer have the spirit to spin.

ᴄHE VOW

On the Chao Phraya River the ferry boatman
whistled with two pinkie fingers
V'd beneath his upper lip
or did he cooee,
or pucker his lips and coo to me
as if we always knew each other?

When I heard his trill
I vowed never to forget him or Thom
who ran past hills of sand or was it coal
and half-built concrete skeletons
on Achar Mean or was it Tousamouth,
where a *cyclo* driver pedaled a woman
with a glazed pig in her lap.

I vowed never to forget how I used
my Swiss army knife
to lop off hunks of gouda,
so he could taste home, how
I smeared Nutella on *numpan*,
baguettes the French left behind
or was it on the sweet flat bread
cooked in a splatter of oil
outside our window.

We drank Nescafé from dusk blue mugs
the size of bowls,
and with a silver teaspoon,
the handle etched with dancing *apsaras*,
later to be mangled by a garbage disposal,
we stirred in sweetened condensed milk
between kisses.

Leaving
Cambodia

Don't mourn for my absence,
but feel my presence
and talk about me.
Postcard from Thom

WHAT IS LEFT

The sapphire ring sticks to my inner thigh,
your father's silver cigarette case squared for non-filters
is cool against my cheek,
the brass chess horse tangles in my hair.
I am a mummy in rolls and rolls of negatives—
photographs I shot of you while you slept,
sweat coating your body in Phnom Penh's swelter.

I bolt awake and grab my journal,
imagine you inside me
and feel nothing.

If I could conjure you to burst through the pages
of the leather-bound book you gave me,
only then would you stop becoming the past.

But you are not here
tearing the pen from my hand,
slamming the book shut.

HAWTHORNE BRIDGE

She did not stand in a sampan and row
with long polls through the muddy Mekong,
but last month she was still living in Cambodia.
Now the bridge is up across the Willamette River
and she is her father's daughter
whose panic kept him from going to the other side.
She does not want to budge.
Even after the bridge pulls itself together,
smooths out its steel hemline,
she will not drive the red rented car one more inch
here, where rain stings like nettles
and has never heard its other name monsoon
whose torrents cup the earth into pools
swelling with lotus pads.

Maybe the honkers will pull her out of the car
and fling her into the river, and
on the way down she can think

Pacific Ocean

carry me back to where memory
and the moment were married

IN A TOWN CALLED SCHNEEBERG

I hide the picture snapped by your wife
for your so-called buddy,
from my new lover—
the picture of you
brown and muscled,
a curl of your black hair sprung free
from the grip of the red bandana
tight across your forehead.
You have shimmied up a signpost
in a whitewashed town in Germany
that announces in big letters:

Schneeberg

You believe that before the Nazis
this town was in my family's pocket.
Your postcard reads, *If you were here,
we would paint the town red*.

THE BELLS OF ST. BAVO SING SCAT

Anticipating the lovers
who will soon be voices with bodies again,
the comforter on the bed fills with light
the color of sky when day puts up her feet and
slips on royal blue slippers.

Outside their window
the man on the roof dangles a dancing bear
or a baby grand or whatever
the lovers want to unhook and haul inside.

Finally, their bodies are fields
of yellow tulips fringed purple
slowly opening their fists,
the bells of St. Bavo singing scat,
fire-breathing dragons barreling out of children's books
to race through the streets of Haarlem.

Belts daddies used for beatings
stay in the loops of their pants.
Charred bodies resurrect themselves noticing
a faint smell of smoke in their sleek hair or
the tweed of their jackets, while lovers
who parted without declaring their love
feverishly lick stamps on envelopes
of yellowed love letters
or claw at blood-red wax seals.

ODE TO A GECKO

My gnome, my *nat*
with sticky pads on your feet,
you three-dimensional sketch,
one black eye in profile,
an Egyptian cat
spread flat, always fleeing
nowhere, hibernator
inside my bedroom walls,

don't abandon me now
that I live in a country of snow
where sorrow resounds
and love is memory.
Let me be you;
I'll slither away
from those who make love and
moan in other rooms.

GRIEF

The sorcerers are bored and frustrated
standing in their glittery robes and pointy hats
in the corner of my parents' small kitchen
where the cupboards never close properly,
the pilot light always goes out, and
my father remains spindly and mute
as before he died.

They kill time rolling small glass balls
in their palms and conjuring
the electric can opener
to delid all the tuna cans,
but finally the incantations and
wand-waving work.

My father is morphing
into his debonair self, tall of carriage
as if a picture were about to be taken
in three-quarter profile, a pipe in his mouth.

He vanishes.
Ashes burn in an ashtray,
the room thick with sweet smoke.

He reappears plumper, but still translucent
holding a bowl with a puddle
of vanilla ice cream and canned peach juice.
He floats down and sits.
The index cards are still
where he left them
waiting for names of uncracked books
and Dewey decimals.

The sorcerers do my bidding
and free him to be
who he never was in life.
Today he knows origami.
Under his hands
library index cards moonlight
as snails, whales, and kangaroos.

The sorcerers are delighted with themselves.
Now, in search of my mother
they squish together for a ride
in the motorized stair chair
my father used at the end.

They find her fast asleep in the den
bent over a crossword puzzle.
When she awakens
all the empty squares are filled-in with:

I LOVE YOU I

L
YOU
V
I WILL ALWAYS LOVE YOU

BEN'S SHOES

Bharata puts Rama's sandals on the red and gold throne.
The shoes remain silent if well pleased.
—*Ramayana*

It seemed like he had hundreds
living in shoe trees,
but the pair she liked best was dressy,
black and smooth as skin.
When she was little, he wore them with a tuxedo
and cummerbund, his hair slicked back.
She was sure he was out dancing with princesses.

Later she understood he was only the hired help,
and that he stood in many kitchens
with others similarly attired
waiting to make an entrance,
holding high above their heads silver trays
ablaze with cherries jubilee.

After she left home
he hung up his cummerbund,
had trouble bending over
and carried a shoe horn in his pocket,
but still polished his black shoes
for the weddings of other people's daughters.

Now she keeps the pair unceremoniously
in a corner of the broom closet,
but like Rama's sandals, her father's shoes
remain regal with disdain,
knocking against each other
whenever she utters a double negative,
forgets to turn off the bathroom light,
or leaves her shoes in the middle of the floor.

LARYNGECTOMY

for Esther Schneberg

They cut out her voice,
like so many before
and after her.
Now others will decide they know
what she is thinking and
will speak for her.
But there will always be the yellow pad,
the spiral notebook,
the loose sheet of paper
by a bed, on an end table,
attached with a magnet to the refrigerator;
the sharpened pencil, the fine-point pen,
the black magic marker hanging from a string
and the words—wise, fierce, raucous
filling up the pages of the world.

INTO MY OFFICE WALKS
VIETNAM'S LEGACY

Portland, Oregon, 1997

With an uncomfortable giggle she says she picked me because she read that ethnic minorities and sexual abuse were two of my specialties and that she fit both categories. Her mother was from Dalat and met her GI father in a bar during the war. When her father was zonked-out on crystal meth, a drug he first procured in Nam, she had awakened to find him on top of her in their camper. There were always empty beer bottles spilling out of the cabinets. She doesn't remember when her parents were not drinking, but her mother did all the smacking, grabbing, slamming, and hurling. The round glass bowl filled with water and her fish the color of a rainbow in gasoline, left a scar below her eye. Her mother swept the dying fish into the trash. *Aren't I crazy calling my parents every week when they never call me?* While she is still young and sexy, she finds a way to make her own money. *American men, stupid and lazy.* Her mother agreed if she looked less Vietnamese she had a better chance. She bought western lids and big bouncy breasts. She is sure she has more repeat customers than the other girls behind the glass booths also touching themselves, because they let drugs ravage their looks, while she ended her orgy with coke six months ago. *Why do I always pick the ugliest boyfriends? I know, because they won't leave me.* She talks about having no women friends, but is scared to contact her best friend in high school, a Mormon, because she wouldn't understand her lifestyle. *I loved going to her house. They all sat down together and put cloth napkins on their laps.* When she went to school, she always did well and could balance a checkbook just like her mother. *I want to get out of the life, but I can't give up the money. Do you think you can help me?*

SUNSET IN HEBREW AND KHMER

I sit and watch the faint pink light
flatten Mount Hood into the sky
and on my lap two books,
one Hebrew, one Khmer.
I go back and forth
between the symbols of the language
that is supposed to be mine
and those of my adopted country.

One holds my pubescence and Mrs. Ribowsky's
Hebrew class, whose wig after she married
looked like Sophia Loren's hair.
She taught me to transform the strokes I saw
as swinging kerosene lanterns, people hanging
onto straps in the subway, outy belly buttons, wishbones
into written language, the characters of my people,
although I light candles only at someone else's Shabbat
and do not believe that g-d is outside or inside me.

The other marks hold my adult daring and
nuns sitting on their haunches sifting dried fish
before mosquitoes descend. Those squiggles and swirls
are trout swimming in pairs, a charcoal burner, tigers' eyes,
the cheeks of a woman way past childbirth
that I will never caress into language.
They will always be above me on stilts
or small candles on toy boats
that will be sucked down the Tonle Sap
away from me.

LEAVING CAMBODIA

August 2000

Seven years later
I am writing in an artist colony,
Tyrone Guthrie's old estate,
at Annaghmakerrig, in County Monaghan.

When words betray me
I walk down a straight path,
past brown cows whose owners' tags
glint in their ear lobes, to smell
the stench of turkeys crammed together,
and to poke huge black bags filled with feed
mulching in farmers' fields.
The drumlins are brutally green.

I drink tea sweetened and milk laced,
poured from squat steel pots
into delicate porcelain cups
with matching saucers and
dine on the last crumbs of my Cambodia,
my stilt home practically abandoned.

GLOSSARY

Achar Mean A main street in Phnom Penh

Angka (Khmer) Literal meaning "organization"—what the Khmer Rouge called itself; Khmer Rouge cadre

apsaras (Sanskrit) Female deities, heavenly dancers, celestial nymphs

Avalokitesvara Lord of compassion, the most venerated bodhisattva

Bagan The monuments of the great Pagan Empire of Burma

BLDP Buddhist Liberal Democratic Party

bodhisattva Individual called to obtain Enlightenment but delays it through compassion for suffering beings

cantonment UNTC requires all factions to turn in weapons.

Chao Phraya River Divides Bangkok

Civpol Civilian Police—U.N. term for its police force from member countries

cyclo (Vietnamese) Bicycle trishaw

Dalang Shadow puppet master

Donchee (Khmer) Buddhist nuns

DK Democratic Kampuchea—Khmer Rouge name for Pol Pot's regime from 1975 to 1979, still refers to the Khmer Rouge.

farang (Thai) Westerner

FUNCINPEC National United Front for an Independent, Neutral, Peaceful, Cooperative Cambodia—Party of Prince Sihanouk

Garuda Mythical divine bird with predatory beak and claws

Irrawaddy River The monuments of the great Pagan Empire are on its banks.

Jayavarman VII (1181-1219) The king considered the greatest architect of Angkor

kechrek A device of metal plates hit by a stick imitating puppet movements, lightning, etc., in *wayang kulit*, Javanese shadow puppet theater

khaet (Khmer) Province

khum (Khmer) Commune

krama (Khmer) Traditional scarf won by Khmers

kyats (Burmese) Myanmar currency

longyis Burmese sarong worn by men and women

luy (Khmer) Money

Mount Meru A mythical mountain at the center of the universe and home of the gods; the axis of the world around which the continents and oceans are ordered

naga Benevolent mythical water serpent

nat Burmese spirit-god

Ne Win Military dictator of Burma from 1962 to 1998. He died December 5, 2000.

numpan (Khmer) Bread

Omtuk Festival Takes place in November. Homage to the moon and the Mekong. Boat races in Phnom Penh on the banks of Tonle Sap and Bassac Rivers

Patpong Road Red-light district in Bangkok

phuum (Khmer) Village

Pol Pot's given name is Saloth Sar. He was referred to by his cadre as Brother Number One

Psaa Tmay (Khmer) New Market

Ramayana An epic classic Eastern love story of good and evil, was probably written by the Indian, Valmiki, between 200 B.C.E. and 200 C.E. Storytellers and writers of Southeast Asian countries, including Cambodia, have modified and built on the original. The story of Rama and Sita and her abduction by Ravana has been depicted in bas-relief at Angkor.
The following are characters and inanimate objects depicted in the *Ramayana*:

  amrta The drink of immortality created by the Sea of Churning Milk

  Bharata Rama's brother

  Chitraratha The Gandharva King is the lord of Heaven's music.

  Dasaratha Bharata and Rama's Father

Hanuman Chief of the Monkey Army

Kaikeyi Bharata's mother

Kausalya Rama's mother

Lakshmana Rama's brother

Lanka Kingdom ruled by Ravana

Maricha The demon transformed into a deer to distract Rama, enabling Ravana to abuct Sita.

Rama The star of the *Ramayana* is the king of Ayodhya and the incarnation of Vishnu.

Rakshasas Demon followers of Ravana who live in Lanka

Ravana The arch rival of Rama and the demon king of Lanka

Sita's husband is Rama. Her mother is Mother Earth. Her father King Janaka found his newborn daughter in a plowed furrow.

Vasuki The rope serpent on which Vishnu sits

rameat thung (Khmer) Bamboo xylophone

riel (Khmer) Cambodian currency

sampot (Khmer) Traditional women's skirt

SNC Supreme National Council—the body and building in which, during the transitional period in Cambodia, the U.N. functioned as government

sout (Khmer) Silk

srok (Khmer) District

Super Great Leap Forward Phrase Pol Pot ripped-off from Mao's Cultural Revolution

thanaka A paste worn by many Burmese women on their faces, made from acacia tree bark

Tonle Sap (Khmer) Great lake. The largest fresh water lake in the country. When the Mekong floods during the rainy season, the Tonle Sap no longer acts like a tributary, but reverses course to become an enormous fresh water sea covering a seventh of Cambodia's land surface.

Tousamouth A main street in Phnom Penh

tuk-tuk (Thai) Motorized three-wheel taxi

UNTAC United Nations Transitional Authority in Cambodia

Yogya Popular abbreviation for Yogyakarta, Indonesia

wat (Thai) Temple

Yuons (Khmer) Derogatory term for Vietnamese living in Cambodia

About the Author

Willa Schneberg worked for the U.N. Transitional Authority in Cambodia from 1992 to 1993, serving first as a District Electoral Supervisor for Cambodia's first "free and fair" elections since the French colonization, registering voters and educating them about the electoral process; and later as a Medical Liaison Officer, supporting the health needs of the seven hundred U.N. volunteers from over one hundred countries. She traveled in Thailand, Indonesia, Vietnam, and Burma during and after working in Cambodia.

Schneberg's poetry has been published by many literary journals, including *The Exquisite Corpse, American Poetry Review, Michigan Quarterly Review,* and *Southern Poetry Review,* and in many anthologies. She has won two Oregon Literary Fellowships, a grant in poetry from the Money for Women/Barbara Deming Memorial Fund, and her second poetry book, *In The Margins Of The World,* was awarded the Hazel Hall/Oregon Book Award for Poetry in 2002. She is a photographer and clay sculptor whose artwork has been exhibited widely. She studied at the Nova Scotia College of Art and Design (Halifax, Canada), S.U.N.Y. of New York at Binghamton, and the Boston University Program in Artisanry with a specialization in ceramics. Schneberg has a B.A. from Empire State College (New York City) and an M.S.S.W. from the University of Tennessee School of Social Work (Knoxville). A native of Brooklyn, New York, she now lives in Portland, Oregon, where she is a Licensed Clinical Social Worker in private practice.

Introduction Authors

U Sam Oeur grew up in a Cambodian farming family. After studying in the U.S., he served in the Cambodian government, becoming part of the Cambodian delegation to the United Nations. When Pol Pot assumed power in 1975, Oeur, along with his wife and son, survived the killing fields while feigning illiteracy in six forced-labor camps. A devout Buddhist, Oeur is the author of the bilingual collection of poems *Sacred Vows*. He now lives in Texas where he translates the poems of Walt Whitman into Khmer. His memoir *Crossing Three Wildernesses* (Coffee House Press), written with Ken McCullough, was released in 2005.

Ken McCullough's most recent poetry books are *Travelling Light* (1987), *Sycamore Oriole* (1991), *Obsidian Point* (2003), and *Walking Backwards* (2005), as well as a book of short stories, *Left Hand* (2004). He has received numerous awards for his poetry including the Academy of American Poets Award, a National Endowment for the Arts Fellowship, a Pablo Neruda Award, a Galway Kinnell Poetry Prize, the New Millennium Poetry Prize, the Blue Light Book Award, and the Capricorn Book Award. Most recently, he received grants from the Witter Bynner Foundation for Poetry, the Iowa Arts Council, and the Jerome Foundation to continue translating the work of U Sam Oeur. *Sacred Vows*, a bilingual edition of Oeur's poetry with McCullough's translations, was published in 1998. Oeur's autobiography *Crossing Three Wildernesses*, written with McCullough, was released in 2005.

Colophon

Text is set in Caslon Old Face
with titles in Dorovar.
Typography by
ImPrint Services,
Corvallis, Oregon.